DATE DUE			
			11/01

Animal Marvels

Reproducing

Please visit our website at: www.garethstevens.com
For a free color catalog describing Gareth Stevens'
list of high-quality books and multimedia programs,
call 1-800-542-2595 (USA) or 1-800-461-9120 (Canada).
Gareth Stevens Publishing's Fax: (414) 332-3567.

Library of Congress Cataloging-in-Publication Data available upon request from publisher. Fax (414) 336-0157 for the attention of the Publishing Records Department.

ISBN 0-8368-2932-8

This North American edition first published in 2001 by
Gareth Stevens Publishing
330 West Olive Street, Suite 100
Milwaukee, WI 53212 USA

© QA International, 2001

Created and produced as *So Many Ways to Reproduce* by

QA INTERNATIONAL
329 rue de la Commune Ouest, 3ᵉ étage
Montréal, Québec
Canada H2Y 2E1
Tel.: (514) 499-3000 Fax: (514) 499-3010
www.qa-international.com

Printed in Canada

1 2 3 4 5 6 7 8 9 05 04 03 02 01

Gareth Stevens Publishing
A WORLD ALMANAC EDUCATION GROUP COMPANY

A high price to pay

Reproduction is a necessary stage in the life cycle of all animals. Animals reproduce to ensure the survival of their species. From the simplest to the most complex, all methods of reproduction are fascinating. Some animals pay a very high price to reproduce. In certain species, animals risk their lives to do the most important thing they will ever do — pass on the gift of life.

A doting father

When the female emperor penguin lays her egg, the male places it on top of his feet and covers it with a fold of skin. Huddling with hundreds of other males in the colony, he keeps the egg warm for over 60 days. When the egg hatches, the female returns with food for her young. Only then is the male free to search for something to eat.

emperor penguin

2

Are you curious?
While the egg is sheltered from the bitter cold of a polar winter, the father penguin has no opportunity to eat. He must live on the fat reserves in his body. The male penguin can lose up to half of his body weight during this fast!

A devoted mother

The female common octopus, plentiful on European coasts, lays nearly 200,000 eggs in clusters that it attaches to rocks. The mother then tirelessly cleans and ventilates the eggs — without stopping for a bite to eat — until they hatch about two months later. After completing this task, the mother may die of exhaustion.

common octopus

A hard life

Atlantic salmon often swim thousands of miles upstream from the ocean to spawn in the river in which they were born. Many do not survive the journey. They stop eating when they reach fresh water. Once their eggs are laid and fertilized by the male, the adults head back to the ocean. The baby salmon stay in the river for a time and then go to sea as their parents did before them.

Atlantic salmon

A long journey

The adult red crabs of Christmas Island live in underground homes away from the ocean. When it is time to lay their eggs, 120 million crabs must take a long, hot walk to the sea. After arriving, those who survive the trip dig holes for the eggs and mate. More than a million crabs die on the difficult journey.

red crab

Male? Female? Neither? Both?

For most animals, reproduction requires a male and a female. Male reproductive cells must unite with female reproductive cells to begin the process. This is sexual reproduction. However, some species have different ways of reproducing. Some animals are neither all male nor all female but are both at the same time. Others do not need a mate. Some even change gender!

Both male and female

Slugs, earthworms, sea cucumbers, and snails have both male and female reproductive organs. When two snails have a sexual encounter, each of them is impregnated by the other. Both partners eventually give birth. Efficiency has never meant so much!

4

common snail

Are you curious?

Human beings have eaten snails since ancient times. The French, who eat more snails than any other nationality, enjoy thousands of tons of these little mollusks every year.

Animals that bud

Several species do not have reproductive organs. Among sponge species, "budding" is a common method of reproduction. That is, a small number of sponge cells gather together to form a reproductive bud. When the "mother" sponge dies, this new bud detaches itself from her body and becomes a sponge in its own right.

yellow tube sponge

clown fish

Male or female?

The clown fish that inhabits the coral reefs and warm seas of the Pacific is both male and female. If the mother clown fish suddenly dies, the remaining fish undergo quite a transformation. The father becomes a female and one of his, or rather her, offspring turns into a male. This enables the family to remain stable.

A female story

Some lizard species are made up entirely of females. When it is time to reproduce, these sisters are capable of doing it for themselves! In the absence of males, the females lay eggs that do not have to be fertilized. All their offspring, of course, are female. Several species of insects, invertebrates, fish, and amphibians also reproduce in this way.

checkered whiptail

Finding a mate

It is easy for members of a species to find a mate when they live near each other. But it's not so easy when they don't. These animals have many different ways of finding each other. Male birds sing; frogs croak in chorus; and mammals low, moo, or bellow. No matter what the signal, it is recognized by members of the same species, sometimes even if they are miles away!

Love songs

During the mating season, the male humpback whale sings love songs that can be heard up to 100 miles (160 kilometers) away! These songs are meant to attract a mate. The male extends his large fins and moves them up and down in time to the music.

6

humpback whale

Are you curious?

Whales do not sing by using their vocal chords. They move air between their lungs, windpipe, and pharynx. The sounds are amplified by the bones in the jaw and the fatty tissue in the snout.

A chemical come-on

Many animals, especially insects, are guided by their sense of smell when looking for a partner. When a female atlas moth wants to attract a mate, she gives off a chemical that is carried away by the wind. The antennae of a male atlas moth recognize the odor of the chemical and the male flies away to be with the female.

atlas moth

Love lights up the night

How can nocturnal insects find each other in the dark? Fireflies have found a way! When it's time to reproduce, males fly over the wingless females that are perched on the ground. They flash their signal lights and the females answer by sending coded light messages. Using these lights as their guide, the males fly to the females.

common English glowworm

Telltale droppings

The female redback salamander found in the forests of North America has a good sense of smell. Entering male territory, she smells the excrement of possible mates to find out its composition. The males with the richest diets are the first to attract mates. Those whose droppings are not so rich must wait a while longer.

redback salamander

Attracting a mate

Some animals go to great lengths to show themselves off to a prospective partner. They use dances, parades, fights, colors, and gifts to charm a possible mate. All these signs of affection are important for another reason. They let members the opposite sex know that the suitor is indeed a member of the same species and that he or she is ready to mate.

A colorful love nest

The male satin bowerbird builds a kind of lane edged with branches. He then stains it with a mixture of saliva and fruit and decorates the floor with flowers, feathers, shells, and berries. This colorful carpet attracts a female, who is then treated to a show by the male. He dances and bows within the nest until she is won over.

satin bowerbird

Are you curious?

There are more than 18 species of bowerbirds throughout Australia and New Guinea. The bowers built by these birds vary from species to species. The males with the least colorful feathers usually build the fanciest structures.

A magnificent display

Birds of paradise are famous for their colorful plumage and for their unusual courtship behavior. The male bird struts his stuff on a branch at the top of a tree. After sending out a resonant call, he lets himself drop down headfirst and spreads out his magnificent tail feathers, revealing a semicircle of beautiful colors.

blue bird of paradise

A wedding present

To win the heart of a mate, there is nothing better than a nicely presented gift. Many animals exchange flower petals, fruits, or even food. The crested grebe engages in a water ballet. The bird dives down into the water and brings up a "bouquet" of seaweed in hopes of pleasing a potential mate.

crested grebe

Savage love

Courtship does not always involve beautiful colors and dances. It can also be cruel and bloody. Some animals engage in battles to decide the choice of a mate. Walrus males use their tusks as weapons to tear at each other's flesh until there is a winner. That male is rewarded with a partner.

walrus

Chance encounters

Some animals do not engage in mating rituals. They just release millions of eggs and sperm into the water. This form of fertilization is called external reproduction. It is common among invertebrates, fish, and amphibians. After the males and females empty their sex cells into water, millions of chance encounters take place. Though the fertilized eggs are exposed to danger, enough eggs survive to ensure the survival of the species.

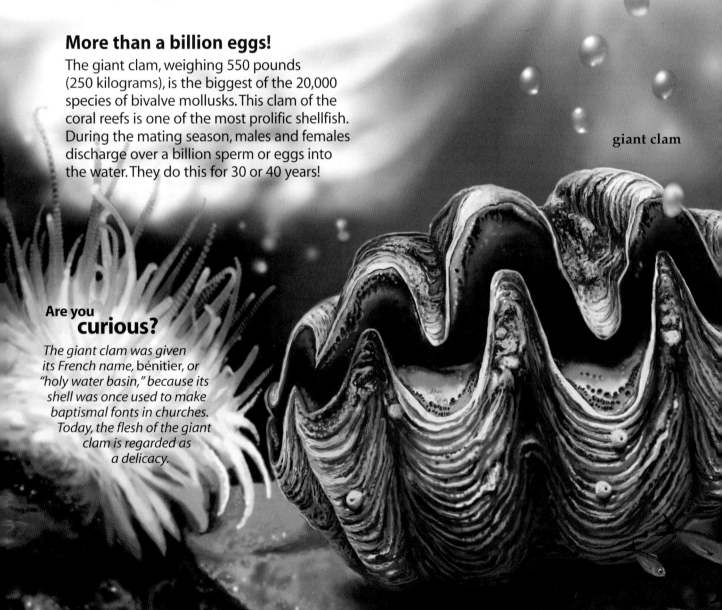

More than a billion eggs!

The giant clam, weighing 550 pounds (250 kilograms), is the biggest of the 20,000 species of bivalve mollusks. This clam of the coral reefs is one of the most prolific shellfish. During the mating season, males and females discharge over a billion sperm or eggs into the water. They do this for 30 or 40 years!

giant clam

Are you curious?

The giant clam was given its French name, bénitier, or "holy water basin," because its shell was once used to make baptismal fonts in churches. Today, the flesh of the giant clam is regarded as a delicacy.

A dazzling spectacle

Australia's Great Barrier Reef is made up of a huge colony of polyps. These tiny animals that make up the coral reef produce many little colorful bundles. The bundles detach and sparkle in a dazzling spectacle, allowing the cells that produce new polyps to join and begin a new colony.

red coral

A fertile embrace

Most frogs and toads mate in the water. Male frogs hold the female in a tender hug that causes her to fill the water with hundreds and hundreds of eggs. The male then does his best to fertilize the eggs. The couple does not leave their embrace until the eggs are fertilized.

common frog

Moonlight mating

Billions of palolo worms live in in tunnels at the bottom of the Pacific Ocean. Once a year, the males and females detach the parts of their bodies that contain the sperm and eggs. These segments then swim to the surface, attracted by the light of the moon. At dawn, this mass becomes a reproductive "soup."

palolo

Close encounters

Mammals, reptiles, and even certain amphibians, birds, and fish rely on internal fertilization to reproduce. Among these animals, no eggs are exposed to outside dangers. The sperm and egg meet inside the female. To make this possible, the males have a specially designed organ. Some use modified parts of their bodies, while others rely on their penises to accomplish this task.

Love on the water

Most male birds have no reproductive organs. There are certain exceptions, however. Ducks, geese, and swans are among the birds that mate on the surface of the water. The male of these species has a penislike organ that emerges from its body during mating.

12

greylag goose

Are you curious?

At birth, baby geese — called goslings — capture the image of the first object they see. From that point on, they consider that object their mother. This is known as "imprinting." Therefore, it is very important that the first object a gosling sees really is its mother and not a dog or a human being!

Loving lions

Lions who are ready to mate begin by rubbing and sniffing each other. During mating, the lion holds the neck of the lioness between his teeth to keep her calm and still. At the tip of the male reproductive organ are sharp little prickles that hurt the female. It is the pain of coupling that causes the female to produce eggs.

lion

Reproductive fins

The torpedo, or electric ray, lives in warm and temperate seas. Two modified fins on its belly serve as a penis. Ridged and rigid, these fins have a small tube that carries sperm. During mating, the male inserts these fins, either together or one at a time, into an opening in the female and then ejects his sperm.

marbled electric ray

A long embrace

Male lizards and snakes have not one but two penises! During mating, these two organs penetrate the female one at a time. On their surface are little bristling hooks that hold the couple together until fertilization takes place. This embrace can last for several hours!

western diamondback rattlesnake

Breaking out

Many animals reproduce by laying eggs. After fertilization, the egg becomes a cozy dwelling filled with food for the developing embryo. Unlike the eggs of fish, which are coated with a jellylike substance, those of land animals are protected from dryness by a shell through which air can pass. Laying this type of egg enabled many animals to leave the sea and live on solid ground.

brown kiwi

A giant egg

The female kiwi bird found in the forests of New Zealand lays one or two eggs a year. Each of the eggs laid by this chicken-sized bird is about 5 inches (13 centimeters) long, 3 inches (8 cm) wide, and weighs 1 pound (0.5 kg), or over one-fifth of the animal's body weight. In other words, these enormous eggs are at least four times as heavy as those laid by hens!

14

Are you curious?

Like ostriches, rheas, and emus, kiwis have tiny wings that do not enable them to fly. Confined to the ground, they have to comb through the undergrowth in search of food for their young.

Eggs on his back

All species of insects lay a huge number of eggs. Most of these tiny eggs can be well hidden in nature, where they are usually abandoned. The female of certain water bugs, however, uses a gummy substance to stick her newly laid eggs onto the back of her mate. He carries them around until they hatch 15 days later.

giant water bug

A tireless protector

Nile crocodile

The female Nile crocodile protects her nest of eggs for four long months. When the eggs are about to hatch, the baby reptiles start making faint noises. The female immediately removes the eggs from the ground and takes them to water, where she helps her young free themselves from their shells.

Egg-laying mammals

Two types of mammals lay eggs — the odd-looking duck-billed platypus and a little spine-covered animal known as an echidna. The female echidna lays one egg a year. She stores it in a pouch on her belly, where it hatches in about 10 days. The offspring stays in the pouch for several weeks, feeding on its mother's milk.

15

Australian echidna

Born alive

Some fish and reptiles, and almost all mammals, produce living young. Among these animals, the body of the female feeds and cares for the young until they are born. Female mammals have a reproductive system that includes a chamber called the uterus where their young develop before birth. An umbilical cord connects the baby to an organ called a placenta. The placenta provides the fetus with nourishment and carries away waste.

Flesh-eating embryos

Tiger sharks complete their development inside their mother's body, where they are nourished by a placentalike organ. Just before they are born, their diet changes. The most fully developed babies start eating their brothers and sisters while still in the womb!

sand tiger shark

red kangaroo

A nourishing pouch

The female kangaroo gives birth to an embryo less than 1 inch (2.5 cm) long. Still attached to an umbilical cord, this tiny being climbs through its mother's soft fur to the pouch on her belly. The baby then attaches itself to one of four teats and begins to nurse, thus beginning the next stage of its development.

Eggs that hatch inside

The young of certain insects, fish, amphibians, and reptiles develop inside eggs, but the eggs are not laid. They remain inside the mother's body. Two to three months after the aspic viper's eggs are formed, they break open inside the body of the mother. She then gives birth to about 10 venomous little vipers.

aspic viper

tailless tenrec

A fertility record

The little tenrec is probably one of the oldest mammalian species on earth. A nocturnal insectivore covered with stiff, prickly hair, it has an amazing fertility record. In a zoo in Holland, a female tenrec gave birth to 31 babies at once! The average tenrec litter is about 15.

Are you curious?

The female sand tiger shark has two uterine chambers. In each of them, one of the baby sharks eats his or her brothers and sisters. At birth, the two surviving sharks are already 3 feet (1 m) long!

Dangerous births

While the births of some animals are fairly easy, those of others can be complicated and difficult. Some newborns have to break out of shells, and some must undertake risky journeys. Many have to face danger, with or without the help of their parents.

Ouch!

The tallest animal in the world has a brutal start in life. The female giraffe gives birth standing up. Her poor offspring falls headfirst from a height of over 6 feet (2 m)! But rather than being shaken up by this experience, the baby giraffe, which is about 6 feet (2 m) tall, spends its first hour of life learning to walk.

giraffe

Mammals born underwater

During the underwater birth of its child, the female dolphin is assisted by one or two other females. One major obstacle must be overcome. The baby dolphin has to breathe very soon after it is born. Because it comes into the world tail first, the females must push it to the surface in a hurry so it can take its first breath.

bottlenosed dolphin

A short life

The leatherback turtle lays and buries its eggs in a sandy beach. After four months, the baby turtles break through their shells, struggle out of the sand, and head for the sea. Their first days of life are far from easy, however, for these tiny babies are preyed on by crabs and birds of prey. Only a few ever reach the sea.

leatherback turtle

An upside-down birth

In several bat species, the mother gives birth while hanging upside down. As soon as it is born, her poor baby must cling tightly to the mother's fur to avoid falling on its head! The Australian flying fox is a bat that gives birth in this way. The baby does not loosen its grip on its mother for two weeks, until it is able to fly on its own.

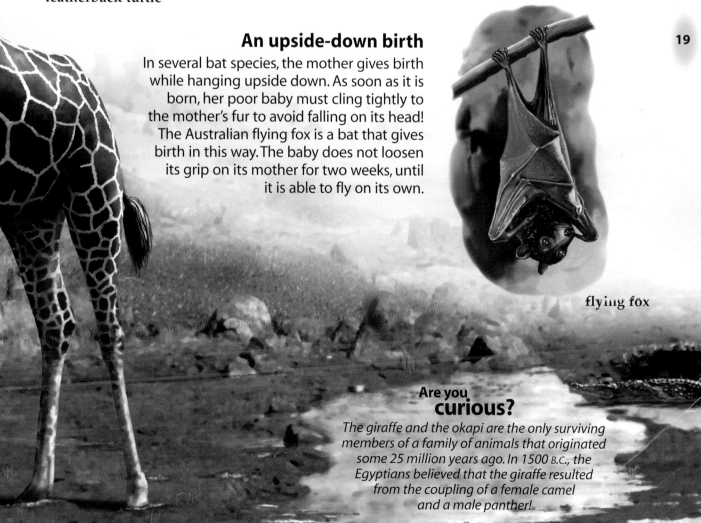

flying fox

19

Are you curious?

The giraffe and the okapi are the only surviving members of a family of animals that originated some 25 million years ago. In 1500 B.C., the Egyptians believed that the giraffe resulted from the coupling of a female camel and a male panther!

Devoted parents

Among many species, parents do everything they can to make sure that their offspring survive. Human beings, other mammals, birds, amphibians, reptiles, and even fish expend an incredible amount of energy raising their young. Immediately after birth, these devoted parents start grooming, feeding, transporting, defending, and educating their offspring.

A female herd

Female African elephants live together in a herd. All are present when a baby, or calf, is born. The calf stays with its mother for several years, but all the females have a hand in its care. If a calf loses its mother before it can take care of itself, it is adopted by another female in the herd.

African elephant

Grooming the little one

Carried for about five months on its mother's soft belly, the baby chimpanzee receives a great amount of attention. In fact, the mother chimp spends much of her day stroking and grooming the fur of her young one. These grooming sessions strengthen the bond between the mother and her baby.

common chimpanzee

A protective mother

Certain fish store their newly laid eggs and the sperm of their partner in their mouth. There, the fertilized eggs develop into young fish. During this incubation period, the female cannot eat anything. Even after they leave their mother's mouth, the baby fish continue to take refuge there at the first hint of danger.

mouthbrooder fish

wood pigeon

Pigeon's milk

Only female mammals can produce milk for their newborns. However, both male and female pigeons have a crop, usually used to store food, that produces a white liquid resembling milk. The parents feed this "pigeon's milk" to nestlings during the first 10 days of their lives.

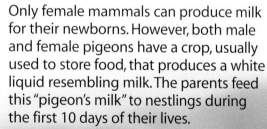

Are you curious?

There are some differences between African elephants and their Asiatic cousins. African elephants are bigger and heavier and have larger ears. Their backs dip, while those of Asiatic elephants are arched.

Abandoned babies

Not all young animals have caring parents. Most insects, reptiles, and amphibians let their eggs hatch on their own. Many animals lay their eggs near a source of food. Butterflies leave their eggs on leaves for the caterpillars to feed on, and flies lay theirs on decaying plants or animals. When the eggs hatch, the babies have something to eat. Most species that abandon their young produce a huge number of offspring to make sure that some survive.

Eggs in termitariums

The 6.5-foot- (2-m-) long Monitor lizards abandon their eggs in the walls of a termitarium. Hidden from predators, the eggs are incubated by the heat of the sand. When they are ready to hatch, a liquid emerges from the eggs, softening the walls of the termitarium so the young can escape.

22

monitor lizard

Adoptive parents

The cuckoo avoids raising its young by laying its eggs in the nests of other birds. When the cuckoo eggs hatch, the newborns throw the other eggs out of the nest. They then get the undivided attention of their adoptive parents! These adult birds feed the cuckoos until they can leave the nest on their own.

European cuckoo

Safe shelter

The bitterling, a tiny fish found in the rivers of Europe, uses a special tube to pump its offspring into the gills of a mussel. The fertilized eggs hatch inside the mussel. Safe from predators, the newborn fish remain in their unusual nursery for about a month.

bitterling

A strange home

The female sheep-nose botfly keeps its eggs inside its body until they develop into larvae. Only then does she inject them into the nose of a sheep! The larvae feed on the blood and sinus membranes of the poor sheep.

sheep-nose botfly

Are you
curious?

The largest monitor lizard, the Komodo dragon, can grow to be 10 feet (3 m) long and weighs about 365 pounds (165 kg). It eats goats, deer, and wild pigs, which it can completely devour in just 15 minutes!

No children

Animals must reproduce to ensure the survival of their species. However, a few animals are not capable of reproducing. They are sterile, meaning they cannot bear young, for a variety of reasons. Certain animals will never be able to reproduce.

Sterile offspring

Two animals of the same species can usually reproduce successfully. Two animals of related species rarely bear offspring capable of living after birth. Some closely related species, such as donkeys and horses, are able to produce young animals called mules. However, the mules will be sterile.

mule

24

Long live the queen!

In honeybee colonies, only the queen's eggs are fertilized. Other bees in the hive include drones, which fertilize the queen, and worker bees, which care for the young, build and clean the hive, and gather nectar. Worker bees are sterile. The queen produces a substance that prevents them from reproducing.

honeybee

What is a steer?

Many human societies have controlled the destiny of certain animals. Male cattle raised for their meat undergo a procedure when they are calves that makes them sterile. These animals, called steers, gain weight and are prized for their meat, but they are no longer able to reproduce.

calf

25

Sterile termites

Only a few termites are able to reproduce. Termite society is made up of reproducers, workers, and soldiers. Only reproducers can become parents. The workers build the dwellings, provide food, and take care of the eggs. The soldiers defend the colony against intruders and take care of the nest.

termite

A map of where they live

More fun facts

NAMES OF ANIMALS AND THEIR YOUNG			
Animal	**Adult male**	**Adult female**	**Offspring**
Domestic	Dog	Bitch	Puppy
	Tomcat	Queen	Kitten
Farm	Billy goat, buck	Nanny goat, doe	Kid
	Buck rabbit	Doe rabbit	Kit
	Rooster	Hen	Chick
	Donkey, jack	Jenny	Colt
	Drake	Duck	Duckling
	Gander	Goose	Gosling
	Stallion	Mare	Foal
	Bull	Cow	Calf
	Boar	Sow	Piglet
	Sheep, ram	Ewe	Lamb
	Turkey, tom	Turkey, hen	Poult
Wild	Bear, boar, he-bear	Sow, she-bear	Cub
	Blackbird	Blackbird	Blackbird
	Buck hare, jack	Doe, puss	Leveret
	Buck, stag, hart	Hind, doe	Fawn
	Bull buffalo	Cow	Calf
	Camel	Camel	Calf
	Bull elephant	Cow	Calf
	Bull whale	Cow	Calf
	Dog wolf	Bitch	Pup
	Eagle	Eagle	Eaglet
	Fallow deer buck	Doe	Fawn
	Fox, dog	Vixen	Pup, cub
	Giraffe bull	Cow	Calf
	Gorilla	Gorilla	Gorilla
	Lion	Lioness	Cub
	Monkey	Monkey	Monkey
	Mouse	Mouse	Mouse
	Ostrich, cock	Hen	Ostrich
	Otter	Otter	Cub, pup
	Partridge	Partridge	Partridge
	Pigeon	Pigeon	Squab
	Rat	Rat	Rat
	Roebuck	Roe, doe	Fawn
	Salmon	Salmon	Salmon
	Snake	Snake	Snake
	Sparrow	Sparrow	Sparrow
	Stork	Stork	Stork
	Swallow	Swallow	Swallow
	Viper	Viper	Viper
	Wild boar	Sow	Squeaker, calf

ANIMAL GESTATION PERIODS

Animal	Gestation period
Opossum	12 days
Mouse	21 days
Rabbit	1 month
Squirrel	1 month, 8 days
Fox	1 month, 24 days
Cat	2 months
Dog	2 months, 3 days
Wolf	2 months, 8 days
Lion	3 months, 16 days
Pig	3 months, 25 days
Beaver	4 months, 8 days
Sheep	5 months
Gazelle	5 months, 10 days
Cow	6 months
Hippopotamus	6 months, 20 days
Bear	8 months
Deer	9 months
Seal	9 months, 6 days
Camel	9 months, 20 days
Dolphin	11 months
Horse	11 months, 5 days
Whale	1 year
Zebra	1 year, 15 days
Giraffe	1 year, 2 months, 20 days
Rhinoceros	1 year, 6 months, 20 days
Asian elephant	1 year, 8 months, 9 days
Alpine black salamander	3 years, 2 months, 20 days

ANNUAL EGG PRODUCTION

Animal	Number of eggs per year
Carp	20
Turkey	70
Clothes moth	200
Hen	300 to 370
Fly	200 to 400
Queen bee	365,000 to 730,000
Queen termite	30 million
Ocean sunfish	300 million

For your information

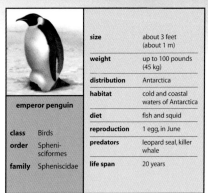

emperor penguin

size	about 3 feet (about 1 m)
weight	up to 100 pounds (45 kg)
distribution	Antarctica
habitat	cold and coastal waters of Antarctica
diet	fish and squid
reproduction	1 egg, in June
predators	leopard seal, killer whale
life span	20 years

class	Birds
order	Spheni- sciformes
family	Spheniscidae

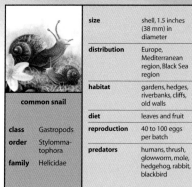

common snail

size	shell, 1.5 inches (38 mm) in diameter
distribution	Europe, Mediterranean region, Black Sea region
habitat	gardens, hedges, riverbanks, cliffs, old walls
diet	leaves and fruit
reproduction	40 to 100 eggs per batch
predators	humans, thrush, glowworm, mole, hedgehog, rabbit, blackbird

class	Gastropods
order	Stylomma- tophora
family	Helicidae

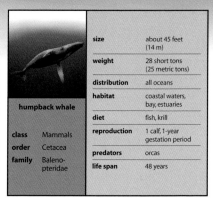

humpback whale

size	about 45 feet (14 m)
weight	28 short tons (25 metric tons)
distribution	all oceans
habitat	coastal waters, bay, estuaries
diet	fish, krill
reproduction	1 calf, 1-year gestation period
predators	orcas
life span	48 years

class	Mammals
order	Cetacea
family	Baleno- pteridae

 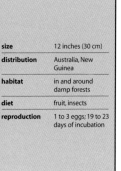

satin bowerbird

size	12 inches (30 cm)
distribution	Australia, New Guinea
habitat	in and around damp forests
diet	fruit, insects
reproduction	1 to 3 eggs; 19 to 23 days of incubation

class	Birds
order	Passeri- formes
family	Ptilonorhyn- chidae

30

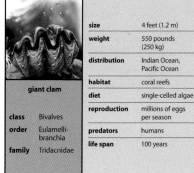

giant clam

size	4 feet (1.2 m)
weight	550 pounds (250 kg)
distribution	Indian Ocean, Pacific Ocean
habitat	coral reefs
diet	single-celled algae
reproduction	millions of eggs per season
predators	humans
life span	100 years

class	Bivalves
order	Eulamelli- branchia
family	Tridacnidae

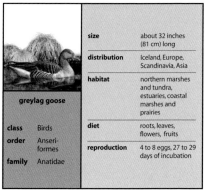

greylag goose

size	about 32 inches (81 cm) long
distribution	Iceland, Europe, Scandinavia, Asia
habitat	northern marshes and tundra, estuaries, coastal marshes and prairies
diet	roots, leaves, flowers, fruits
reproduction	4 to 8 eggs, 27 to 29 days of incubation

class	Birds
order	Anseri- formes
family	Anatidae

brown kiwi

size	about 26 inches (66 cm) long including beak
weight	about 7 pounds (3 kg)
distribution	New Zealand
habitat	forests, thickets
diet	insects, spiders, earthworms, fruit, seeds, leaves
reproduction	1 to 3 eggs, incubated for 75 to 84 days by the male
predators	dog, cat, opossum, weasel
life span	at least 10 years

class	Birds
order	Struthioni- formes
family	Apterygidae

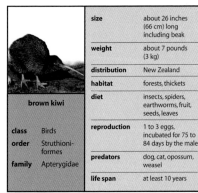

sand tiger shark

size	10 feet (3 m) long
distribution	Atlantic Ocean, Indian Ocean, Pacific Ocean
habitat	shallow bays and coastal waters
diet	cephalopods, crustaceans, rays, small sharks
reproduction	2 baby sharks at a time

class	Fish
order	Lamniformes
family	Odontas- pididae

giraffe

size	up to 18 feet (5.5 m) tall;
weight	up to 2,000 pounds (910 kg)
distribution	Africa
habitat	savannas and open areas
diet	leaves; acacia and mimosa shoots
reproduction	1 baby giraffe; 15-month gestation period
predators	lion, panther, hyena, African hunting dog
life span	25 years

class	Mammals
order	Artiodactyla
family	Girafidae

African elephant

size	up to 11 feet (3.4 m) tall at shoulders
weight	up to 6 short tons (5.4 metric tons)
distribution	Africa
habitat	forests and savannas
diet	branches, twigs and leaves
reproduction	1 baby; 22-month gestation period
predators	lion (hunts baby elephants)
life span	55 to 60 years

class	Mammals
order	Proboscidae
family	Elephantidae

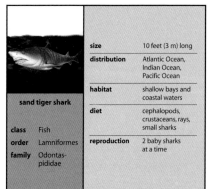

monitor lizard

size	over 4 feet (1.2 m) long
distribution	Africa
habitat	forests, open areas, along rivers
diet	fish, small vertebrates, crocodile eggs
reproduction	up to 30 eggs
predators	humans, large carnivores, birds of prey, crocodiles
life span	up to 30 years

class	Reptiles
order	Lepido- sauria
family	Varanidae

mule

size	5.5 feet (1.7 m) at the shoulder
weight	up to 1,600 pounds (726 kg)
distribution	China, Mexico, South America, Africa, North America, Europe
habitat	mountains, deserts, semi-arid regions
diet	grass, hay
reproduction	sterile
predators	wolf

class	Mammals
order	Perisso- dactyla
family	Equidae

Glossary

abandon: To leave without intending to return

amphibian: An animal, such as the frog, that can live on land or in water

amplified. Increased, augmented

burrow: Hole an animal digs in the ground for shelter

carnivore: A plant or an animal that feeds mainly on meat

code: A system of signals used for communication

colony: A group of animals that live together as part of a community

coral reef: A ridge of limestone made up of coral skeletons

courtship behavior: The set of movements an animal makes to show that it is ready to mate

dwelling: A place that can be inhabited by a living being

embryo: A stage of development following the fertilization of the egg

estuary: An arm of the sea

fertilize: To unite a sperm and an egg to begin the development of a new individual

functional: Capable of fulfilling the required function, or suitable for the task needed

gestation: The period during which a female carries her offspring before birth

incubate: The process of warming an embryo so that it can hatch when the time is right

insect: Any of a class of arthropods that includes bees, beetles, and crickets

insectivore: An animal or plant that feeds mainly or solely on insects

invertebrate: An animal without a spine

larva: An often wormlike form that is one stage of an animal's life

limestone: Rock made up mainly of calcium carbonate

mammal: A member of any animal species in which the female has mammary glands for feeding her young

mollusk: An animal with a soft body that has no bones but usually has a hard shell

offspring: All of the children or young of a human being or an animal

pharynx: The canal between the mouth and the esophagus

placenta: An organ that provides a fetus or an embryo with nourishment and carries away the

embryo's waste; it is connected to the fetus by means of an umbilical cord

plumage: Bird feathers

polyp: An animal with a hollow cylindrical body

predator: An animal that destroys or eats another

reproduction: The function that allows a living being to produce another being or beings of the same species

reptile: A crawling animal with scale-covered skin, such as the snake, the iguana, and the tortoise.

ritual: Rules, gestures, and actions that recur regularly or are repeated more or less the same way

savanna: A treeless plain

species: A class of related organisms

temperate: Moderate, referring to a climate that does not have extreme temperatures

termitarium: A termite's nest

trachea: A tube or a canal that conveys air from the larynx to the bronchi; windpipe

tropical: Relating to or occurring in a frost-free climate with warm temperatures

ventilate: To expose to air

Index

32

Editorial Director Caroline Fortin **Research and Editing** Martine Podesto **Documentation** Anne-Marie Brault **Page Setup** Lucie Mc Brearty
Illustrations François Escalmel, Jocelyn Gardner **Translator** Gordon Martin **Copy Editing** Veronica Schami **Gareth Stevens Editing** Joan Downing
Cover Design Joel Bucaro, Scott Krall